VALLEY OF WANT

VALLEY OF WANT

Ross White

Poems

Copyright © 2021 by Ross White
All rights reserved

First printing

Paper   ISBN 978-0-87775-075-8
Cloth   ISBN 978-0-87775-076-5

∞
This text of this book is printed on Mohawk Via. This paper is acid-free and meets ANSI standards for archival permanence.

Unicorn Press
Post Office Box 5523
Greensboro, NC 27435
unicorn-press.org

Distributed to the trade
by Small Press Distribution
of Berkeley, California

VALLEY OF WANT

1	Here Be Monsters
2	This Garden, If Only I Could Neglect It, Would Not Have to Be a Garden
4	Self-Portrait with Single Malt Scotch and *Guitar Hero*
5	After the Party
7	I Say Ice
8	If You Are So Eager to Be Hated
10	Performativity
11	There's a Void and It Needed a Villain
12	Illness Narrative
14	Iridocorneal Endothelial Syndrome
16	No True North
17	Expert Advice for Living a Full and Happy Life
19	Iridocorneal Endothelial Syndrome
20	This May Be Worth Preserving
22	"If I Have Not Talked to You in a Year, I'm Deleting You"
24	Mission: Impossible
25	Shoreline with Decaying Wildlife
26	Perennial After Winter
28	Ladybugs
30	Valley of Want
31	Aubade with a Line from Julia Kolchinsky Dasbach

HERE BE MONSTERS

At this longitude, land disappears into a tail,
a serpent with forked tongue,
scales, eight muscled legs.

Here be the unexplained mysteries
of the universe. Here be the shimmering truth
of claw and wretchedness.

Ships cannot help but sail around capes
to arrive in the mouths of beasts.
Sailors cannot escape their dark eyes.

Here be the unmappable,
the crags and cliff faces of something
gloomy and afflicted.

Here be the stories we tell ourselves.
Here be the stories we tell ourselves
we need to survive.

THIS GARDEN, IF ONLY I COULD NEGLECT IT, WOULD NOT HAVE TO BE A GARDEN

This cardinal perched
            in the willow can't stop
     being a cardinal perched
in willow and this blue jay
          in the cedar is,

     when I relent to the real,
overwhelmingly, a blue jay in cedar.
            The house no longer smells
     of lavender or cardamom.
Cornhusks mold

           in the thirteen-gallon kitchen
     trash can. Perfumed
in their spoilage,
          I will sleep fitfully tonight.
     The dun hours

before sunset I'll waste
          with my hands in soil,
     pulling thistle and selfheal
at the root to make room
          for other roots,

     the ones that exist now
only in the version
          of the world I imagine
     for myself, a version
to which I return

> when I discover the real
> to be common ragwort,
> blooming alkaline
> and bitter in its beds.

SELF-PORTRAIT WITH SINGLE MALT SCOTCH AND GUITAR HERO

Alternately, Self-Portrait on a Wednesday Night.
Alternately, This Keeps Me from Engaging
with a Friend Who Continually Disappoints Me.
Alternately, I Hardly Leave My Basement.
Alternately, The Soft Forest of Carpet
Beneath My Bare Feet Will Suffice as Refuge.
Alternately, If I Could Shrink Myself and Wander
Its Great Fibrous Oaks, I Might Never Regret Solitude.
Alternately, Self-Portrait with Thunder In My Bones.
Alternately, I Got into an Argument Over Drowning,
and Whether a Drowning Man's Twitch Might
Be Misconstrued as Dancing, to Which I Replied,
Clearly You've Never Seen Dancing, to Which
She Replied, Clearly You've Never Seen a Man Drown,
to Which I Replied, I Have and I'm Him Now.

AFTER THE PARTY

What confetti litters the grass
has blown away by noon.
An overturned chair suggests
nuisance rather than revelry.
The amps buzz their impatience
for new sound but no guitar
is plugged in. The empties
practically scatter underfoot,
the wrappers shimmer
ugly in the sun.
No one's coming to clean
the mess. No one's coming
for years. By the time
it gets talked about again,
vines will have grown thick
around the table legs
and high grasses will obscure
Coke bottles and faded signs.
And when someone startles me
from the apiary I'll quietly
tend, when someone reminds me,
I won't remember any of it
as a party. I'll remember it
as a butterfly garden full
of dead monarchs, a
cask of vinegar. I won't think
it was fun. I'll hear
once more the firecrackers
that kept the neighbors
restless and enraged,
I'll remember the night

when, careless and wounded,
I suffocated
a lightning bug in a jar.

I SAY ICE

with this mouth and I say
        disappointment. I say universe
and cosmos and I say earthbound
        and stasis. My tongue smashes
its way into calamity and my lips
        split over virgin or bourbon.
I say ice with this mouth
        that's already melting: abscesses
and spices in the sores.
        Salts. I say salts and the crystals
clip the sloughy skin behind
        my traitor lips. I say ascension
and this mouth hardly believes it.
        These things I say are prayers
and pleas and please until they
        answer themselves unanswered.
I say lies and lies. I whistle
        sometimes but am stuck saying
when the whistle doesn't work.
        Sure I'll click and moan with this
mouth but I say ice and transgress
        too with this mouth and I say
flight and I will rise. I set goals
        with this mouth and soon
I say more lies. I say
        my surrender. I say ice
with this mouth as if to explain.
        I say earthbound and stasis.
I say disappointment.

IF YOU ARE SO EAGER TO BE HATED

someone in America is always hating.

Like a doughnut shop that lights its neon
to beckon the hungry, & later, the staggering drunks,

hang your shingle & whip up a fresh batch
of business cards. You needn't wander far

into the countryside before the grasses of intolerance
rise to the knees. Every city & township

has an I Don't Understand You Rd. intersecting with
I Hate What I Don't Understand St.

The poet Nazim Hikmet said, "Outside the door
is the whole bustling world...my fellow patients,

we'll get well." He believed in the palliative:
a sycamore would bloom, the tallow would burn

bright through the darkness, & we'd be cured.
But need for a cure implies a sickness. We don't talk

about that ache—but sometimes we boil the sheets,
sometimes burn the beds. Hikmet didn't need

to manufacture an enemy. For him, it was enough
to ponder love without dousing himself in bleach,

without hiring goons to smack him to the pavement.
For some of us, cruelty arrives predictably,

like a train in peacetime, in the form of our own aging
hands, our calcified hips, & we curse nothing more

than time & our own failures. But if you crave
it, cruelty has a stadium full of fans,

mostly young men with cropped, fine hair,
who readily stiffen their arms in salute

& cheer the team onwards toward victory.

PERFORMATIVITY

you see me, I know, you eye me, you scan
columns of me and rows within the columns,
you click photos of me and clock my doings,
I know, gawk at my breakfasts, peep me,
load me to get a load of my most recent
outsized feeling—a rail against injustice,
a barb toward the president, a hint of unnamed
sickness I let slip, oh God it's exhausting
showing all this—I know you empath so hard,
tap Like or Heart to project your regard
for my bravery (necessary to dole out, like scoops
on a cone, the harm befalling me daily),
I know you strength me, you sorry that happened
me, you sending a hug me, it's never enough
to shutter the factory, inside me is industry
manufacturing miseries, your clicks the coal,
your eyes the turbines, you engine me, assembly me,
repackage and label me, distribute me,
where once the world brambled me (the tear
not so deep, no more than a scratch), you salve
the wound with oils and honey and milk
and sometimes well-intentioned salt
and hashtags and *bravery bravery bravery*

THERE'S A VOID AND IT NEEDED A VILLAIN

I hate the word "lovers," its farce
        as a too-intense moniker.
What passes for love is often just a volcano,
        a sweatshop, an overheated engine.

I say things all the time to overstate my case,
        as if argument were a form of glue
but opposition a kind of lubricant
        at a time when I'm desperate not to fall apart.

"Lovers" sounds a lot like "lemurs"
        but lemurs become quite comfortable in captivity.
A good lover cannot quite be trapped,
        or if confined, will rattle the cage,

too unruly to be properly cared for.
        The temptation is nonetheless great.
When I stare at glowing ember atop ash,
        I always imagine wrapping my palm

around the fleeting pulse of its orange.
        Every good idea needs a companion.
In captivity, lemurs adapt to use tools,
        a behavior never seen in the wild.

They need constant stimulation.
        The tools prevent tension and aggression.
The moment after you called me "lover,"
        I could sense myself becoming its opposite:

a damp towel, a submarine, a truncheon.

ILLNESS NARRATIVE

Because I am horrible,
I don't care about your illness narrative.
I am sick myself. Of myself. & so magnolia
hurls its white blossoms toward spring,
& so the weevils stain the cotton
with their young. Take this new scarf,
this crude wooden figurine of a long-nosed troll.
My lungs are dark & stringy, contaminated
by the nearby, listless heart. & so fishermen
wrench pollock from the sea & walleye
from the river, & so pails fill with milk.
Tell me a story that doesn't end
in senseless trauma. I don't care
what you have to go through
to conjure it. & so the godwits
thrust their bills into the black shore,
& so the grackle's black feathers
stain blue skies seeking a friendly branch.
It is easier to invent than to listen.
Through the window, I see the world
wondering how to stun us all
with its magnificence but everywhere
the wounded are walking & talking.
& so the anchors find the waiting seabed,
& so the moon rides up on its dark chariot.
Tell me that story, the one where night
lifts its lesser stars & strokes them
like pets, & the incensed sun lashes
its reflection to a hunk of rock

revolving around earth. & so
all shadows will be reminders, enough
sometimes to make me feel loved.

IRIDOCORNEAL ENDOTHELIAL SYNDROME

The ocean of my eye was on fire. Ships crossed
its oily channels. Though it was hazy, I could see captains
christening their mahogany bows with champagne,

I could see, just barely, the shores on which their wives
and children and grandmothers waved handkerchiefs,
I could see smoke rising from blue waters.

Western stars gave them bearings, eastern stars
gave them something to hope for as they slid
across the maddening surface. I wished for their rudders

to puncture the cornea, the iris, anything:
Oh, I wanted blood. I wanted confirmation
running down my cheeks that I was damaged.

So many people rushed to give me assistance when I got sick
and none asked me *What is it like?* The needle scared me less
than the prospect of never meeting someone

similarly affected. Not blind, though certainly
that was a possible future. Just alight. The cornea
a funhouse distorting every image, the iris stretched like lycra.

I was a midshipman waiting for an admiral to make sense
of the course that had been charted for me.
I searched for a white whale but I never had a glimpse;

maybe he was never there. Maybe there was no reason,
maybe smoke forgot its blaze. I want so much
for illness to be sensible, but there is no sense. Some of us

are whole and then we are not whole. Ships sail
into inferno. A few land in darkness and report back:
darkness. A few land in paradise and report back: *darkness*.

NO TRUE NORTH

or stars to guide the skiff.
No wind to draw its sail.
And though I see shore,
or imagine its outline
on the horizons, the waiting
hovers like a dragonfly.

I should honor the gulf
between where I am
and where I want to be,
but where I want to be
is years ago, and the salt
water I bail each night
from the bilge I find
each morning in my canteen.

EXPERT ADVICE FOR LIVING
A FULL AND HAPPY LIFE

Get drunk every day. Punch a wall every day.
Throw rocks every day. Rocks at squirrels and mice.
Steal something every day, at least that's what
Dorianne Laux said, something small and hopeful.
Play poker every day. Gamble away a fortune
every day. Make something terrible every day,
with your hands. Not violent, mind you, but
terrible, the kind of bad parents hang on refrigerators,
the kind of bad that cracks in a middle school kiln.
Throw up every day. Shoot a rifle at the constellations
every day. Accuse them of being too close.
They are, those stars, too close. They see something
in you no terrestrial body can see. But it's there,
in you, because you feel it every day. Do what
you can to suppress that part of yourself,
and if it must come out, channel it into wickedness
that hurts no one but you. Victimless crimes,
they'll call what you do. Isn't it lovely to not have
a victim? To not be a victim? Get wise
every day. Feed the cat every day.
Fold laundry every day, even the fitted sheets.
Send a postcard or a text to a friend every day
with a dumb platitude or a rude drawing.
See how long you can make the cat believe
you're a good person. Then your boss, your wife,
your priest, your yoga teacher. Chain the days
together like days without an accident,
red Xs on a calendar, until they number
in the hundreds, the thousands. Get old
every day. Do your stretching, take your statins,

trim your nose or ear hairs every day.
You'll die from it, all of it, but no one
will tell you that you can't. Can't die like that.
Look in the mirror every day, and dismiss
all that horrible. All that horrible, you can see it.
The constellations can smell it on you.
The squirrels and mice know. The rats.

IRIDOCORNEAL ENDOTHELIAL SYNDROME

Why am I wasting daylight, I wonder,
looking out the window at ocean so blue
Renaissance painters struggled to capture the color.
This is what I do now, when one eye scabs over
like a patient in gauze. I fret about what I cannot see,
I fret about the way light dims and eventually fades.
The whitecaps stream by, uncontent to live out their days.
I could walk toward that ocean, I could dive in
and open both eyes to the salt, which would help
the weakening eye, leeching out fluid trapped
under the cornea. For many years, my doctor thought
I was just photosensitive. Each time I am submerged
in darkness I worry I will not be able to return.
I stay inside. I watch the waves crash and drag
the sand back to some unknowable depth.

THIS MAY BE WORTH PRESERVING

Maybe because I'm older I no longer fear
hoary monsters under the bed,

I hold snakes in roughly the same regard,

and am more frightened by an ulna
snapped in the greasy light of an x-ray.
I know now what hurts in ways I didn't.

I also know the goldfinch at the feeder,
a few back-porch beers with baseball
on the radio, growing lamb's ear in planters,

waking on the afternoon couch to find
I've drooled generously during my dream
of being a sasquatch ripping through
glinting lake ripples on a jet ski,

duct-taping an undersink pipe
to stave off a repair bill, discovering
obscure garage bands on thrift-store vinyl,

realizing I've dived headfirst into water
too shallow but not snapped my neck.

If the body fails me now, its joints
creaking and its poor neck cracking,
its withering liver sputtering out
unruly alkalines, so be it.

I remember what loss does to a heart.
I remember what loss does to a heart

that hasn't been fed. Here is a tablecloth,
and here a bib. Take them with you
into forest lined with *No Trespassing* signs.
Take them with you as you navigate

rapids roaring white over centuries
of rock that never smoothed.

"IF I HAVE NOT TALKED TO YOU IN A YEAR, I'M DELETING YOU"

says the woman my wife maintains a tenuous Facebook friendship with.
And I know this isn't much different from a "new phone, lost contacts"
situation but I'm struck by how easily she thinks a person can be deleted.

My first love lied when she said she was assaulted in our classmate's van.
Through two years of college she maintained that lie
and told me she'd kill herself if I ever left her. That was twenty years ago

and I thought about her on a windy beach today, as a helicopter
delivered Santa to a tourist resort. The sand flew at my eyes
like vengeful spirits in campy movies, and suddenly, I found myself

salt-stung and wistful for the first person who ever intentionally hurt me.
It had been years—honey-thick and wave-beaten years—since I'd thought
about that lie, which for so long I carried on a hunched back, through mountains

and into estuaries, as though I'd never divest myself of its weight.
Forget what Bishop said—the art of losing was a bitch to master.
I had been desperate for oblivion if it meant I could leave the past

in the past. I extinguished so many candles hoping I could forget what light
looked like. I snuffed them with fingers, with ragged breath.
I wish I'd been supportive of every woman who'd told the truth about a man

and his bare ego but that lie was a vestment, a cloak I didn't know
I was wearing. And when I took it off, I shed so much of my past in snakeskin.
Left it behind in the grasslands. But when I did it, the canvas was ebullient white,

the kind of blankness Zen monks would cut off their fingers to experience.
The only cost to forgetting that lie was forgetting so many other things—
street names, classmates, the scent of yellow roses in Reynolda Gardens.

And forgetting too much of what came after—the chatter of redbirds, a sea
of applause from a crowd in Tennessee, the plaque we hung in memory
of someone lost. I kept the shapes like silhouettes, like photo negatives,

occasionally like chalk outlines. But now that my wife's Facebook friend,
who she hasn't seen in more than a year, is deleting the people
she hasn't spoken to, which means my wife is about to be deleted,

I find myself wanting to hold onto everything. To remember it all.
The scent of her honey shampoo. Bags of chips she hoards
in the bottom shelf of the pantry. The way, when she concentrates,

she splits her fingers on her forehead like Mr. Spock
when he says *Live long and prosper*. I could be one betrayal, one wrong
breath from a careless stranger, away from losing all of this.

Right now, she's sitting across from me, reading my friend Nina's book
about feeling like an alien in the place where you live. I'm trying to memorize
the curl of her hair against her shoulder. To moor this moment

in my heart, indelible, impervious to whatever will delete us,
whoever decides we're not on the list worth keeping.
Each day someone I love posts that they have lost someone they love.

MISSION: IMPOSSIBLE

I never until now understood the allure of Hollywood the unsettling need
to be someone else to be for a few hours an international spy for a few others

a young woman in a terrible remote cabin but since I've felt numb to the joys
of rhododendron of walking a path through sweetgum and spruce

I've come to accept that escape is a function of doubt do the sweetgums escape
do the spruces or maples do they dream themselves into the bodies of foxes

traipse through the forest admiring their legs pluck cherries and swallow
the whole pitted fruit does the spy in the movie when the projector flickers off

dream of being a barber or filing his taxes does the young woman bleeding
her way through the forest when she's finally vanquished her grizzled attacker

dream of being a waterfall would you call that escape my mother calls from Colorado
to tell me to meditate she says I want you to be present I'm not present I say

already drifting into time I climbed a mountain in West Virginia to its peak
sat crosslegged just listened the sound of the mountain was no other sound

but my heartbeat I was for a moment the mountain but mostly I'm numb
to the joys of nuthatch song red columbine wild pumpkin I watch movies

I'm trying to remove all obstacles to joy trying like a spy in my own body
to infiltrate the morning trying like the fox dreaming of becoming a placid lake

SHORELINE WITH DECAYING WILDLIFE

Dead jellyfish littered the beach,
their stinging tentacles drawn inward.
Sand flies congregated on their translucent skins.

Further down, I saw a dead brown duck,
its head turned up so awkwardly I wondered
what could have snapped its drawn neck.

In its oily feathers, I could almost see the veins
of a crocus leaf. Its eye shimmered with cold,
luxurious void like anthracite, like prayer.

I thought a lot about forgiveness on that walk,
I thought a little about my own complicity
in a world that would just as soon break me.

Seagulls descended, screeching their chorus
of need, and I strained to smell the ruin
they must have smelled, its sour ethyl.

I wanted it to enter my nostrils like incense.
Underfoot, shells crumbled and I felt the sting
of chitin against skin, but I did not limp.

PERENNIAL AFTER WINTER

If I have failed at loving the world—
oleander in its pinwheel glory,
the bright orange belly
        of an oriole at the feeder,
white mulberry catkins catapulting pollen
        at half the speed of sound!—
it is because I forget sometimes to forgive myself.

So permit me the work
        of rejoicing,
permit me sap in my throat turning to song,
frost on my fingertips followed by the scald
        of warm water reminding them of joyous touch,
rubies in my cheeks as I warm,
tamarind and wind and bud and sled.

I am not ready to love unconditionally
but will, in whatever season you let me,
take a crowbar to the ungrateful barn
        in my heart in hopes
that dew on the aster
or a backyard fire under clear sky
        might empty it.

Permit me, shadow self
        that stalks like a lion on savannah,
respite from your gargoyle whisper
and give me time. I have done so much

wrong that the body will be slow
        with remembering,
and I will accept this slowness,
as I might accept a collar, a leash—

a reminder at my throat.
So when the rupture of dahlia
        or the suddenness of crape myrtle
one day stuns me into serenity, it will be in full view
        of cruelties and calluses past,
the lion hunched and inert,
        content to strip gristle from old bones.

LADYBUGS

Your friends think it cruel that the nickname
you gave your wife can be shortened to, simply,
"Bug," cruel that you've used that nomenclature
for years, but one autumn a loveliness of ladybugs—
those convex miniature volcanoes—tiptoed
their pussyfooted ballets over the bedroom walls,
the ceiling, the jersey bed sheets, and split
their hard shells, brandishing reedy wings
and buzzing with flight only when you attempted sleep,
so you lobbed an arm like a hand grenade
over your also-awake wife, and gossiped
until almost dawn the way you both did
when love was so new you could barely restrain
the urge to name her a million different, lovely names.
How could you have killed a single ladybug
that night, knowing karma is quick to unholster
its six-shooter on any slight? But when you,
haggard, dull, sighed your way through the rest
of the week's workdays, you'd be damned
if you would find the red pests lovely again,
so you shortened the nickname, and there
it has stayed for decades, despite
that fine collective noun, a loveliness of ladybugs!
Imagine, as so many insects receive pejoratives—
plagues of locusts, clatters of spiders,
scourges of mosquitoes—you had stumbled
unconsciously toward the one bug which,
when congregated in a bedroom or in infinite sky,
was described so generously:
it was as if your lady's voice was the beating
of those wings until that night when those wings

beat so loudly, and in your red desire for sleep
you pondered cruelty toward your little visitors,
an unkindness (ravens) that cast so long
a shadow (jaguars) that in the black afterimage
you could feel murder (crows) in your heart,
until finally you were ready to leave all nouns,
all sense, behind. Still, you needed a name
for her loveliness, so blazing and buzzing
it also sometimes kept you up at night,
so you settled into a word that might have repulsed
the neighbors, her co-workers, but which came
to you like she did—as swarm, as unstoppable hum.

VALLEY OF WANT

      I want & want & the moon
          keeps blazing
              orange in night sky.
Coyotes keep baying
          to the gods who hide
                the rabbits.
              Like
lemmings & town drunks,
          waterfalls keep throwing themselves
              aqueously
          over cliffs & I want.
Mushrooms tip
      their purpling caps
          as if daydreaming &
      through all descending mists
I want & want. What
      hunger. What salute
          to desire
is this paddock in darkness,
              swelling with the guttural urging
                of toads &
            symphonic creaking
      the grasshoppers saw
          from the teeth
          of their legs.
I want all nights to be this
      night & all nights to ache
      with this want &
I want & want
    & how
      & how could I not.

AUBADE WITH A LINE FROM JULIA KOLCHINSKY DASBACH

And if you find in your heart a stint,
if joy suffocates and the blood is still thick
as liquor when you look out the window
to the sun—

if you see in its rising only new rage,
as a hammer sees only the stud—

then I gift you this photograph:
your hair dyed red as a cherry, thumbs loose
in twin shaka signs, wearing a t-shirt
so stupid I won't, or can't, repeat it here.

You were happy once, or whoever
took the photo must have thought
you were happy in that moment—
a look like you'd never made a list
of disasters.

Coal ash spills into the cool river of morning,
turkey vultures descend on a split possum.
Underneath a precarious tanker,
whales swallow plastic.

Go on, exhaust yourself before the coffee
drips into your mug.

I'll wait.

And I'll counter with this:
before you woke, a hummingbird like the phantom
of loss crashed toward the feeder
you hung beside the window,
and I skimmed with the back of my hand
your shoulder.

When I pulled away, you said
More.

The following poems appeared, sometimes in earlier forms, in these journals:

Barrow Street "Ladybugs"
BOAAT "After the Party"
Crazyhorse "Performativity"
DMQ Review "Mission: Impossible"
Indianapolis Review "Self Portrait with Single Malt Scotch and *Guitar Hero*"
Moon City Review *"There's a Void and It Needed a Villain"*
Sundog Lit "I Say Ice"
Third Wednesday "Shoreline with Decaying Wildlife"
Thrush "Illness Narrative"
Tinderbox Poetry Journal "Here Be Monsters"
Zocalo Public Square "Valley of Want"

"Self-Portrait with Single Malt Scotch and *Guitar Hero*" was nominated for *Best of the Net 2019* by *Indianapolis Review*. "I Say Ice" was nominated for *Best of the Net 2021* by *Sundog Lit*.

Thank you to everyone who helped these poems find their final forms or provided necessary inspiration along the way: Kate Arden, all the Bread Loafers, Michael Broek, the entire Bull City Press family, Sara Burge, Gabrielle Calvocoressi, Maria Isabelle Carlos, Carrie Chappell, Kelly Copolo, Julia Kolchinsky Dasbach, that wonderful extended Frost Place family, Jennifer Givhan & Molly Sutton Kiefer, Raye Hendrix, Marlin M. Jenkins, David Jibson, Annie Kim, Dorianne Laux, Michael McFee, Matthew Olzmann, Emily Rosko, Sean Shearer, Natalie Solmer, Noah Stetzer, Rosalynde Vas Dias, Helen Vitoria, Connie Voisine, C. Dale Young, the Lindanians, and all the wonderful participants, too numerous to name, from The Grind Daily Writing Series. My dazzling students, you fill me with such hope and joy. Dilruba Ahmed, none of these poems would have found their way into the world without your careful eye and generous heart. Andrew Saulters, for your tenderness and extraordinary care, I am forever grateful. Miss Ladybug, you let the loveliness continue to swarm, and I am still looking for the words.

Ross White is the author of *Charm Offensive*, winner of the 2019 Sexton Prize, and two chapbooks, *How We Came Upon the Colony* and *The Polite Society*. His poems have appeared or are forthcoming in *American Poetry Review*, *New England Review*, *Ploughshares*, *Poetry Daily*, *Tin House*, and *The Southern Review*, among others. He teaches creative writing and grammar at the University of North Carolina at Chapel Hill and directs Bull City Press. Follow him on Twitter: @rosswhite.

Text and titles in Fairfield.
Text design by Andrew Saulters.
Cover design by Ross White.

100 hardbound copies and
400 copies bound in paper
were produced by hand
by Unicorn Press.